# Prisoner Inside My Heart

*"Bring my soul out of prison that I may praise Your Name."*

...King David

Written By
Juanita Lubin

## Dedication:

To The Lord Jesus Christ who came to heal the brokenhearted, to proclaim liberty to the captives and recovery of sight to the blind, to set at liberty those who are oppressed. We honour Him today as we continue His work of setting the prisoners free through His Mighty Name.

# Acknowledgments

It is difficult to acknowledge everyone who has spoken into and had input into my life. There are many mentors, teachers, and friends who added a piece into the puzzle of life, thereby making it take on shape and form. As well as renowned teachers and authors, there have been friends, who have co-laboured along the way, and we have all learned together. There is not room to list everyone but you know who you are and I am eternally grateful. Thank you for your gifts of knowledge and your valued friendship:

*John & Paula Sanford, John & Carol Arnott, Neil Anderson, Jack Frost, Betsy & Chester Kylstra, Mary Audrey Raycroft, Mary Fulton, Will & Madeleine Walker, Faith Robinson Baczko, Eeva Jallo, Laura Nelson, Linda Kearney, Tuesday Cell Group, Laurie & George Hull, the late Bessie Snow who was my first mentor and my parents, John and Sarah Saunders who first modeled life lessons to me.*

© Copyright 2012 — Juanita Lubin

**Jael's Lighthouse Publishing**
**Toronto Canada**

All rights reserved.
This book is protected by the copyright laws of Canada.

This book may not be copied or reprinted for commercial gain or profit.

This book or portions thereof may not be reproduced stored in a retrieval system or transmitted in any form without prior written permission of the publisher.

All scripture quotations, unless otherwise indicated, are taken from the New King James Version®. Copyright © 1982 by Thomas Nelson, Inc. Used by permission. All rights reserved.
Scripture quotations marked (AMP) are taken from the Amplified® Bible, Copyright © 1954, 1958, 1962, 1964, 1965, 1987 by The Lockman Foundation. Used by permission." (www.Lockman.org)

ISBN: 978-1475085020

Email: jaellighthouse@gmail.com

# Contents

| | | |
|---|---|---|
| Introduction | | 8 |
| Chapter One | Identity & Destiny | 11 |
| Chapter Two | Judy – *New Age Nightmare* | 19 |
| Chapter Three | Sarah – *Bullied Into Submission* | 29 |
| Chapter Four | John – *Mistaken Identity* | 36 |
| Chapter Five | Rebecca – Voiceless & Unheard | 46 |
| Chapter Six | Carolyn – *Disappointment With God* | 55 |
| Chapter Seven | Jim & Joanne – *Marriage on the Rocks* | 61 |
| Chapter Eight | Rose – *The Victim* | 68 |
| Chapter Nine | Dianne – *Aborted Hope* | 79 |
| Chapter Ten | Sonya – *Sex Slave Survivor* | 88 |
| Chapter Eleven | My Route to Freedom | 99 |
| Chapter Twelve | Personal Workbook | 102 |

# Introduction

We all occupy spiritual space and we determine which zone we sit in by what is happening inside our hearts. We have all made a choice for the throne zone of God, or the enemy's home. *What zone are you living in?*

Ephesians chapter 2 verse 6 is very clear about our positional authority in Christ, however, the enemy has lied to us and because of the covenant we make with him, through our agreement with his lies, we are living far below our royal status.

I have ministered around the world for the past 20 years through teaching and counselling, and found a common factor in people seeking help. They are all prisoners inside their own hearts.

The enemy has dug out a well deep inside their hearts, built supporting walls of bricks called self protection, capped it with an iron cover of shame and made it his hiding place, his throne zone. He has placed a "No Trespassing" sign on top and we are fearful of going there, because we do not want to deal with the feelings we buried so long ago.

The enemy established this stronghold for himself and has put up some flags warning us to keep out. Self protection, Hiding, Fear, Shame are some of the most common signs that appear in the enemy's throne zone.

As Christians we can often quote scripture describing our authority in Christ, but those scriptures just bounce off the iron cover of the well where the enemy remains hidden from our view. We will never successfully remove this stronghold until we first identify, and then destroy the hiding place of the enemy.

Having ministered to children as young as 6 years of age and men over 80 who spoke very little English, I had to create a way to communicate which was easy to understand. This was necessary in order to facilitate their receiving the healing God so desired for all of us to experience.

As children we first learned by looking at objects or pictures, and the identifying information was filled in by our parents, so we could associate the picture with the word we were hearing.

Therefore the picture and the word **dog** went together in our minds. We learned the word and it branded an image in our minds. Later in school we hopefully learned how to spell it correctly!

Jesus understood this principle because He often used parables, which were picture stories to teach his listeners life concepts, as He spoke to them. While preaching or teaching I found that we can teach the truths of the bible, but those truths are best remembered by people when you give them a living example of what you are telling them.

So if I wanted my listeners to remember a truth, I would always paint a picture with word stories to seal the truth in their minds. Once, I was teaching a message of obedience being a matter of the heart's focus and my dog Princess was busy nursing her first litter of pups at the same time.

She became the object lesson for my sermon, as I described her strong will and refusal to go for walks prior to becoming pregnant with her first litter of pups. In fact I did not take her for a walk but for a drag, as she was always digging in her heels, refusing to be led anywhere.

Following the birth of her pups, walks became a pleasure as she would be single focused in her desire to get out, get her business transacted and get back to her babies. Her heart focus had changed and it led her to obedience. I therefore believe that the best way to understand the principles and concepts that I want to teach you is by giving living examples.

The stories on the following pages are a composition and mixture of the various people I have ministered to worldwide. I pray that their healing journey will lead you to finding your path to freedom from the pain within your own heart. Stories and names have been changed to protect and cover others. May you be blessed!

*Juanita Lubin*

## Chapter One

# *Identity and Destiny*

Jesus said, "I have come that they may have life, and that they may have *it* more abundantly." (John 10:10b). He wasn't talking about when you get to heaven. He meant for you to have and experience a full life here and now on terra firma. Your feelings and beliefs stop you from living what God intended for you, but the truth sets us free.

There are several <u>key questions</u> every person must ask themselves at some point in their lifetime. Without the correct answers to these questions, we will never truly know God's plan and purpose for us.

**Question 1: What is my true identity** - Who am I?

Knowing your true identity is vital because it shapes:

- **Your Sense of value and worth** - Do I matter? Do I have value? Am I worthy?

- **Your Belief system** – What you really believe and why.

- **Your Behaviour patterns** - How you behave.

**We all live our <u>identity</u> through what we <u>believe</u>.**

You can tell me you believe something with your mouth, but I will tell you what you really believe by what you do and how you act. Your actions determine who you are.

- If you are bitter, your attitudes and actions will be bitter.

- If you are an angry person, your words and actions will reflect that.

- If you believe you are a failure and will never amount to anything, you won't.

So if you are living out of a false identity, it is affecting every area of your life. God wants to change that. Health, wholeness, prosperity, and meaning in life come from knowing who you are. Unfortunately some of us are prisoners inside our own hearts.

**Question 2:   What is my DESTINY** - Where am I going?

A sense of destiny gives <u>purpose for living</u>. It answers the questions: Why am I here? Where am I going? What is my life all about? Does my life and where I am now have any significance in God's eternal plan?

<u>Without a sense of purpose</u>, life has little or no significance or meaning. It feels pointless and this is the place the enemy loves us to be in as he can bring in apathy and passivity - (hopelessness). God wants to change that as He is the God of all hope.

**Question 3: What is keeping me from my destiny?**

The answer is usually deception by the enemy or ourselves. Satan is the father of deception. If we knew we were deceived we would no longer be deceived.

**Satan wants to imprint** messages on your heart such as:

1. You are nothing. You are nobody. You were born the wrong sex.
2. You are rejected, not wanted, not loved, not included.
3. You are a failure; you don't have what it takes to succeed.
4. You are stupid, ugly and undesirable.

He wants your identity to be based on his lies which are hidden **in shame, fear and rejection**. He desires to rob you of your destiny and uses every opportunity to sow these messages into your heart. These messages act as curses over our life.

**God's message is just the opposite:**

1. You are loved. You are precious. You are special.
2. You are supposed to be here. You are chosen

3. You have a purpose and destiny that no one else can fulfill.

4. You are the only one that can accomplish what God has placed you here on the earth to do.

These Godly messages are blessings. When we bless others we impart identity and destiny into them. God or Satan uses people to impart identity and destiny into our hearts. They both use people who have influence over us such as: parents, family, teachers, bosses, co-workers, church leaders and members, friends, and spouses. These people have been ambassadors for God or Satan and have either blessed us or cursed us with the words of their mouth.

**Proverbs 18:21A -** *"Death and life are in the power of the tongue."*

**Question 4: Whose report have you believed and how has it defined your life?**

Remember, we live our identity out of what we believe in our heart.

**Your identity may be formed from:**

- **A Lie** - Other people have lied to you about who you are. They said or implied through their actions, that 'you were not wanted', 'you are unworthy', 'you are stupid', 'you are unattractive', and 'you are a disappointment'.

- **Shame** - You were shamed, ridiculed, or humiliated in front of others by the actions and words of influential people in your life.

- **Rejection** - Because of experiences with being rejected, you believe that you will always be rejected. You have taken it on as part your identity.

- **Fear** - When your trust has been violated, fear becomes a part of you in the form of mistrust. Fear is the opposite of faith and without faith you cannot please God. The word of God is hinged on that truth – Psalm 118: 8 states:

*"It is better to trust in the LORD, than to put confidence in man."*

This scripture is the exact midpoint mark of scripture. We must always remember there are no coincidences in scripture.

- **Performance** - Your identity is in what you do and how well you do it. Your identity is based in your **job,** your **role,** or, what your spouse or father does.

In addition to your identity being formed from the words, actions, and experiences of life; your responses of anger, hate, bitterness, shutting down emotions, rejection, control, and fear help shape your character. You agree with the lie "This is who I am and what life is all about." You then tolerate and live with a lie as if it were the truth.

When we live with a lie we have entered a covenant with the devil. One of his names is the *father of lies* (John 8:44), so if we believe a lie we have come into agreement with him. He is the father of deception and will keep us deceived if possible.

God is the Father of All Truth... *"And you shall know the truth and the truth shall make you free."* (John 8:32) Further along in John 14:6 Jesus said *"I am the truth,"* so truth is a person. When we invite Jesus into our hearts he comes in and fills every area that we surrender to Him.

Unfortunately, the devil has carved out a hole in our heart through the prior wounding of life, and has enthroned himself there. He knows he has taken legal ground in our hearts, by our agreements with the lies we believe. Because God granted us free will, the devil is entitled to reign in that area of our heart, until we break our agreement with him.

It is as if that part of the heart is unredeemed, and has no knowledge of its position of authority and immunity in Christ. Thus, when we get into challenging and stressful situations in life, the one responding is that child within, who was taken captive by the enemy through his lies.

King David knew about that according to Psalm 142:7 where he cried out to God – *"Bring my soul out of prison, that I may praise Your name."* Your soul consists of your mind, heart and will.

My prayer is that as you read through the biographies in the subsequent chapters, you will identify with the individuals and their stories of how God healed them and set them free from captivity. My desire is that subsequently you find your own freedom by working through the Personal Workbook, a user friendly guide at the end of the book.

# Chapter Two

## *Judy* - New Age Nightmare

Judy a frail timid woman, sat on the edge of the sofa as we shared a cup of tea and she told me her story of a life of abuse and neglect, first by her parents and then by her husband. As a child of four, she had been sodomized by her step-father while her mother was away at a Christian conference. Because she believed that Jesus was not there to protect her, she hardened her heart to all Christian things and fulfilled her spiritual need in the realm of the new age where she practiced and participated in many of its disciplines.

Now a single mother with three young children, she had long ago given up her relationships with new age associates and had sought refuge in the faith of her mother. Her mother had been the only solid rock of support though her 30 years of running from God.

Judy had been involved in some hard core aspects of the new age. She had channeled demonic spirits, masquerading as the dead relatives of clients seeking her for help to work out their unresolved grief. She had even graduated as a Reiki master and had also done psychic surgery on some clients.

Judy's presenting problem when she came to seek counselling was that she was having nightly demonic visitations and often felt the presence of evil around her which she constantly had to fight off.

As I ministered to her, the truth of her step-father's offence came to the surface and with the help of the Holy Spirit we were able to discover and expose the hiding place of the enemy. Judy left with a tremendous sense of freedom and deliverance that day. She discovered the lies which she believed had become the stronghold the enemy used to keep her in bondage.

The following is the model we used to identify and expose the walled city inside Judy's heart. With the help of The Holy Spirit, Judy identified the core lie that was hidden behind her belief system and that was - *God could not help her.*

The emotions by which Judy ran her life did not correspond with her faith. When Judy first became a believer, she truly did understand what she was doing by making a commitment to Christ.

She understood what the scriptures meant about being born-again, but after a few years of being a Christian, the demonic torment began. She first fought it off with all the fervor and optimism of a new convert, but the years of relentless torment had worn her down and she had fallen into agreement with the enemy that *God could not or would not help her.* Her agreement just opened the door further to the enemy.

The counsellor opened the scriptures and pointed out to her that there were truths in the Word of God that we need to agree with by faith in order to walk in freedom. Some of the truths Judy knew, but when it was presented to her that day it finally made sense to her. The written Word became alive to her.

In the **Word of God** it speaks about **its** own power to heal and free us. The following is what THE WORD has to say about HIMSELF:

> **JESUS CHRIST is the eternal Word that became flesh.** John 1:1-3

*¹"In the beginning was the Word, and the Word was with God, and **The Word was God**. ² He was in the beginning with God. ³ All things were made through Him, and without Him nothing was made that was made."*

In verse 14 of John 1: **The Word** becomes **Flesh**   *"And the*

Word _became flesh_ and dwelt among us, and we beheld His glory, the glory as of the only begotten of the Father, full of grace and truth."

> ## The Word of God accomplishes the reason for which He sent it. Isaiah 55:11

"So shall My word be that goes forth from My mouth; It shall not return to Me void, But it shall accomplish what I please, and it shall prosper in the thing for which I sent it."

> ## The Word of God exposes/reveals our condition.
> Hebrews 4:12-13

"For the word of God is living and powerful, and sharper than any two-edged sword, piercing even to the division of soul and spirit, and of joints and marrow, and is a discerner of the thoughts and intents of the heart. And there is no creature hidden from His sight, but all things are naked and open to the eyes of Him to whom we must give account."

> ## God sent us His word and healed us (past tense).
> Psalm 107:19-20

19"Then they cried out to the LORD in their trouble, and He saved them out of their distresses. 20 **He sent His word and healed them,** and delivered them from their destructions."

> ## Curses can afflict us if there is a legal right.
> Proverbs 26:2

"Like a flitting sparrow, like a flying swallow, so a curse without cause shall not alight."

Therefore according to these scriptures, curses without a just cause cannot attach to us, and if they do, we have authority to stop it. The enemy cannot afflict us unless there is fertile ground belonging to him. The opposite of this truth is that the enemy has a legal right to attack us if we have an open door as a result of sin.

The sin in our life attracts demons as surely as accumulated garbage attracts rats to our house. So, if we don't want an infestation of rats, mice and other vermin in our house we have to take our garbage to the curb. We get to decide what we live with.

The legal rights of the enemy to attack us can come from two sources:

1. Our own sin
2. The iniquities of our ancestors.

The word **sin** means an act, thought, or way of behaving that goes against the law or teachings of God's Word, or falling short of His mark; whereas,

The word **iniquity** is from the Hebrew word *avown*, and means to flow in a certain way, or bend under pressure, or have a fault line. A fault line is a hidden structure defect that will cave in under pressure.

The gravitational pull of the moon on the earth will shift fault lines under the earth's surface and cause earthquakes which can devastate cities.

A fault line in our generational lines can cause devastation in our lives if not dealt with; because the enemy knows where to put pressure on us to sin in the same areas as our parents. The iniquitous roots of our family bloodline can be an open door for the enemy and we can be suffering with reaping the harvest for the sins sown by our ancestors.

> **The <u>Word</u> instructs us of our legal position and rights.**

## **<u>Our Position</u>**

Right now we are spiritually seated in heavenly places in Christ according to Ephesians 1:19-23.

### **Ephesians 1:19-23**

*19 "and what is the exceeding greatness of His power toward us who believe, according to the working of His mighty power 20 which He worked in Christ, when **<u>He raised Him from the dead</u>** and **<u>seated Him at His right hand in the heavenly places</u>**, 21 far above all principality and power and might and dominion, and every name that is named, not only in this age but also in that which is to come. 22 And He put all things under His feet, and gave Him to be head over all things to the church, 23 which is His body, the fullness of Him who fills all in all."*

### **Ephesians 2:4-6**

*"But God, who is rich in mercy, because of His great love with which He loved us, 5 even when we were dead in trespasses, made us alive together with Christ (by grace you have been saved), 6 **<u>and raised us up together, and made us sit together in the heavenly places</u>** in Christ Jesus."*

## **Our Legal Rights**:

We have absolute authority over the enemy according to Luke 10:19.

**Luke 10:19**

"Behold, I give you the authority to trample on serpents and scorpions, and <u>over all the power of the enemy</u>, and nothing shall by any means hurt you."

Although Judy had been raised by a Christian mother, the iniquity in her step-father's line had affected her. Her step-father had been molested as a boy by his older brother and subsequently, because of his wounding, molested her.

Judy's reaction to his sin against her only led her away from God, her true source of healing and comfort. Her wounding caused her to believe lies about herself, others, and God, and she made judgments and vows as a result.

At the first session with Angela, her counsellor, Judy had discovered the lies that she had run her life on for many years.

The following are the lies she believed, as well as the judgments and vows she made as a result:

- I am a victim, I am helpless (a false identity)
- God did not love me enough to protect me

- Others can use and abuse me and I suffer the consequences, while they escape without punishment (a judgement)
- I am unprotected and vulnerable therefore I have to protect myself. (vow)
- You cannot trust men, they will hurt you.

As Judy finally articulated the lies that had come from the wounding of her childhood, the counsellor showed her how the enemy of her soul had dug a deep well in her heart and built himself a stronghold in which he was securely enthroned.

Using a single sheet of paper, the counsellor drew the form of a heart on the paper; next, she put a circle in one corner of the heart and put a throne inside the circle. Outside the heart and just below it she then drew a little box and put a sad face inside it. Above the heart she drew another throne.

See Diagram on following page:

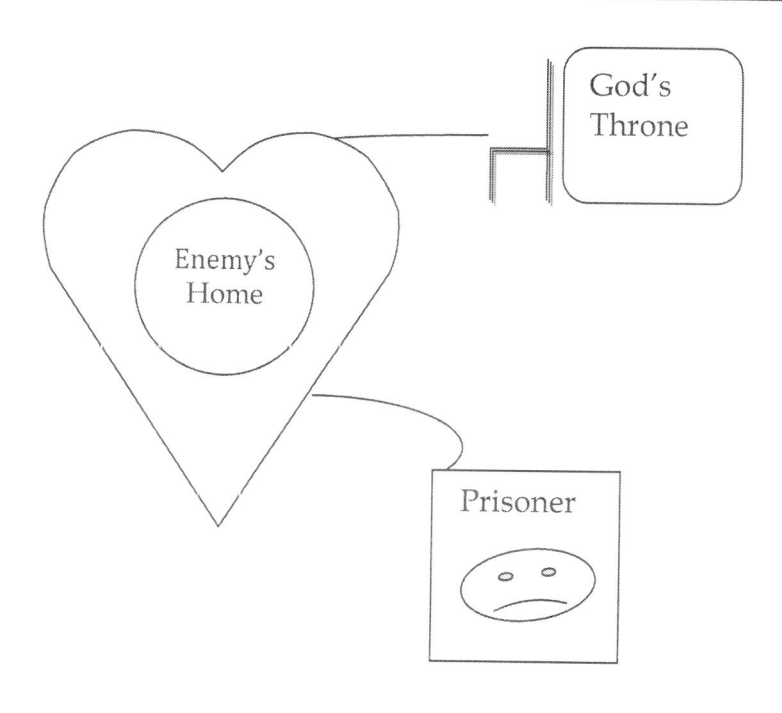

[Diagram: A heart shape labeled "Enemy's Home" (inner circle), connected to "God's Throne" (box at upper right) and "Prisoner" (box with sad face at lower right).]

She went on to explain how the lies Judy believed had given the enemy a legal right to come in and make his home in the injured part of her heart. He had established his throne in her heart on top of the lies she had believed, as well as the judgments and vows she had made. He had therefore taken her captive and she was imprisoned by her own agreement with him. The counsellor explained that emotionally she was trapped at the age of four when the offense had occurred.

Therefore, locked inside that prison was the child who had been molested, and then imprisoned within the lies, judgments and vows she had made as a result. That is why she reacted like a child emotionally when she was triggered by similar events in her life.

The counsellor asked her at what age she had accepted Jesus as her Lord and Judy told her that she was 35. Next the counsellor told her that when she became a believer, Jesus came in and filled every part of her heart that was available for Him to fill, but He could not enter the stronghold of the enemy, because of the agreement Judy had made previously with the father of lies.

Judy then found out that her road to freedom was to break agreement with the lies she believed, and the subsequent judgments and vows she had made. Next she asked The Lord to come into that wounded place in her heart and dethrone the enemy and kick him out. The counsellor led her in a prayer of confession, repentance, and forgiveness. For the first time in 30 plus years Judy felt free.

## Chapter Three

# Sarah – Bullied Into Submission

Sarah stared blankly at the woman who sat before her. Tears were stinging the back of her eyes and the lump in her throat could not hold back the waves of emotions washing over her body as shame, fear and anger struggled to take control. She had sat in this chair many times, only in different locations, and with different counsellors, trying to help sort out the pain of her life.

Somehow today was different. It was as though the woman had laid an axe to the roots of her self-protection, and Sarah could no longer keep everything stuffed behind the good girl façade she has worked so hard to maintain for most of her life.

The counsellor had in one sentence, just laid Sarah's soul bare, and she felt completely exposed and vulnerable. She lowered her eyes and looked at her hands, because the knowing look and love that came from this woman was unbearable.

Sarah had hidden in a world of escapism and fantasy most of her adult life. She had found comfort in the fact that when life got too difficult, she could fold herself away inside a new character or adventure to escape the reality of her wounded heart. When Sarah was 10 years old her parents had moved from the country into the city and she was forced to join a new school in the middle of the school year. Sarah was small for her age and there was one larger girl in her class that took merciless delight in bullying Sarah to the point of fear and tears.

Sarah became the victim of this abuse every day of the week and longed for weekends to escape to the safety of home and her latest book. During the week she would stay in the classroom and read to avoid the playground and the incessant bullying.

One day the teacher confronted Sarah and told her she was not permitted to remain in the school during recess periods, but had to be out in the fresh air and sunshine with the other children.

Sarah manipulated every moment of her school day to avoid the continual harassment, and sometimes she was successful in avoiding her tormentor. As often as she could, she would leave the playground to go to the bathroom and remain there hidden until recess was over. Most of the time, however, she found herself in circumstances where she would have to remain passive to avoid the abuse.

Due to this learned behaviour of passivity, Sarah became the perfect candidate for an abusive marriage. She met her husband Bill just as she was entering her eighteenth year.

She was enthralled with his take charge manner and felt so protected when she was with him. By the time Sarah was nineteen, she was married and expecting her first child. The real Bill turned up just after her first child was born and his true beliefs of the duties and responsibilities of women and men within marriage became clear.

Bill had been raised by fundamental Christians who had majored in a biblical misinterpretation of submission. Sarah had slowly come to the realization that she was trapped in a marriage where she felt more like a slave than a soul-mate, wife or mother.

Sarah was 10 years into her marriage and expecting her fourth child when a sense of hopelessness crept into her life and she had come to the point where she was ready to walk out on her relationship and go it alone with her children.

Her old friend Mary had dropped by one day for coffee and Sarah was shocked at the difference in Mary since the last time they had done coffee a few months previously.

Mary told her that she had invested into her own well being, and sought a counsellor to help her get to the root of some of the issues which kept her from fully enjoying her life and relationships.

Mary went on to explain that the counsellor she saw was unlike any other counsellor she had visited in the past. This woman was not satisfied with giving advice but wanted to get to the roots of why Mary felt and thought the way she did.

She focused in on the lies that Mary believed and how those lies had been formed inside Mary. Mary told Sarah that this woman had told her that each lie is rooted in an emotion. The example the woman had given Mary had the same effect on Sarah as Mary retold it to her.

"The counsellor gave me the example that we often feel or sense rejection not just think it. When we suffer from rejection we go through life with a sense of expectation that others will reject us.

We often don't even think about it, we just feel it. This lady told me that having a lie inside you is like having a rock in your heart with a string attached to it, and at the top of the string in our mind is a balloon with the lie hidden inside.

## Feeling – Thinking Connection

(What I feel in my heart is hidden in my thinking)

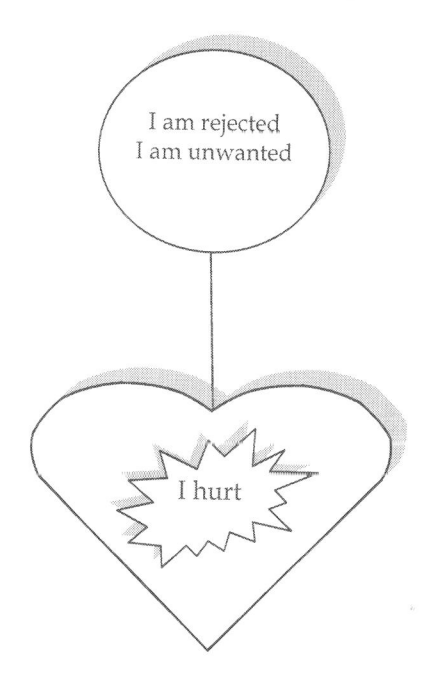

```
   ⭕ I am rejected
      I am unwanted
        |
        |
      ♥ I hurt
```

"With her help," Mary said, "I was able to identify the name of the rock, and also the lies I believed about myself or others, as well as about life itself." "The most interesting thing," Mary went on to explain, "Is that our beliefs are connected to the hurtful and wounding times in our life." For example, I had not been in relationship with Peggy for two years because she had a party and neglected to invite me. You know Peggy and I were very close at one time and it hurt me that she left me out."

"Well, after I had my counselling, I went to Peggy to ask forgiveness for my snubbing her continually and explained why I did it. She told me that the party she had with her other friends was to discuss an upcoming project that she knew would bore me to pieces, so she chose not to put me through the pain.

She apologized for not being more explicit in her previous explanation of why I was not invited. Our relationship is now mended and the most amazing thing is that I am no longer offended by like circumstances because the root of my rejection has been healed."

"The interesting thing is the root was not the problem with Peggy, but my sister Harriet, who would continually leave me out of her groups when we were children. I have believed the lie, 'People close to me reject me' since I was 5 years old. Imagine going through twenty years of believing a lie. But the counsellor told me that she deals with sixty and seventy year olds that have the same problem. I'm just glad that it didn't take that long for me."

After Mary left, Sarah thought about what Mary had told her and eventually called the counsellor's phone number that Mary had left with her.

Sarah found herself, sitting in front of the same counsellor who had just helped her unpack the suitcase of lies, judgments, and vows she had struggled to carry since her experience in primary school.

The core lie that Sarah believed was that *'when life gets too difficult, I can escape the pain through fantasy'*.

That was precisely what she was doing in her life at present. Books, TV, and movies were her preferred avenues of escapism, but sometimes she would find herself just sitting and staring into space not knowing where her mind had been. It was as though something had grabbed her mind and she just exited life for a time. With four small children, she knew she could not continue to do this and that is why she had sought help.

Over the next few visits Sarah was able to come to a place of healing through forgiveness, and deliverance from the escapism she had chosen as a way of protecting herself from reality. By isolating her judgments and vows, she was able to adjust her thinking and make changes to confront the real issues in her marriage, her victim and predator thinking.

With the help of the counsellor, her husband was also able to find freedom from his wrong thinking.

Following individual counselling, they were then able to receive joint counsel regarding their marriage relationship. Currently they were seeing great improvement from their former relational problems.

## Chapter Four

## *John* – Mistaken Identity

John could not stop the convulsive emotions flooding through him as he finally for the first time told the secret he has locked inside for the last 40 years, since he was a 5 year old child. He had spent many Saturday afternoons hanging out next door in the garage with Mr. Hanes as the old man worked on his car. John's dad always worked at the office on Saturday and mom was busy cleaning house, so he had lots of time on his own. Mr. Hanes had taught him the name of the different car parts as he fixed them. He had always considered Mr. Hanes to be his best friend until the day his best friend betrayed him.

Looking back, he still does not know how the terrible incident happened and he did not remember when the warm embrace of his friend turned to the perverted touch of molestation.

He had heard his own spirit scream inside for it to stop, but he was fearful that he would disappoint this person who has become the father figure he so desperately needed in his life. His own dad did not have the time to spend with him because he was always busy at the office, often coming home after John was asleep, and leaving in the morning before he got up.

As John told his story to the counsellor, he could still smell the car grease from the old man, and his stomach churned as nausea washed over him. That day was the day that John lost his innocence and his trust of others. He had pulled inside and hid his real self from the world. He had stayed away from the old man for a few weeks, but his need for a father just drew him back Saturday after Saturday despite the horror and pain he would endure. The abuse had come to a sudden end when the old man dropped dead of a heart attack, one day before Christmas.

John mourned the old man for a while and because he had started middle school, he began to develop new friends and soon put all memory of the abuse to the back of his mind.

In high school John developed a close relationship with Phillip who was a member of the Boy Scouts, just like John. Once when they were on a sleep over together, Phillip approached him sexually and John found himself complying. Later as Phillip slept, John lay thinking that he must be gay because this is the only kind of relationships he was experiencing. John had several same sex relationships over the next 10 years and had decided that God has made him this way.

He would have continued in his lifestyle had he not met Joan. Joan was unlike any woman he had ever known before. She made him feel like he could conquer the whole world to be with and protect her, she made him feel whole and complete as a man.

Joan was his best friend and he fell completely in love with her, and after 2 years of dating they were married. For several years they had a wonderful relationship, but Joan was now pregnant and having problems with the pregnancy. John was fearful of anything happening, so kept his distance sexually from his wife.

He had come to seek counsel because he found that he was looking at other men with more interest than a passing glance. He was fearful that he was being drawn back into his old lifestyle and did not want to be unfaithful to his wife and soon coming son.

During ministry, the first incident with Mr. Hanes washed to the surface, and as it did, so did the truth of what he believed during that time.

John believed there was something wrong with him because his own dad did not want to spend time with him. He also believed that people in authority would abuse and use you. He believed, he was dirty and disgusting and no one would love him if they knew what he was really like.

He felt that he could never really trust those close to him as they might betray him. He believed He was gay and no woman would want him. He also believed He was a victim and had no right to establish healthy boundaries. He believed that God was there that day and did not protect him; so as a result, John decided he would become his own protector. The way he had accomplished this was to stuff all the hurt and pain deep inside, and pretend it never happened. This is called repression and when people do this, they often forget themselves what really occurred.

John sat there with all the memories flooding back and he was finding it difficult to maintain control. Tears welled up in his eyes and a wave of shame mixed with release washed over him as he cried for the loss of the innocence of that little boy.

When all his emotions were spent, the counsellor gently asked him if he was willing to forgive. He drew back in anger at the suggestion. She went on to explain that when we won't forgive, we are giving the predator or perpetrator the legal right to still hold us in captivity. It is like we are handcuffed to the person in the spiritual realm, and everywhere we go, they go with us. When we forgive, we take off the handcuffs and go free.

She also went on to explain, we don't have to feel forgiveness in order to give it. We can give it through an act of our will. Forgiveness is not permission for the person to abuse us again, nor is it necessary to be in relationship with the abuser, if they are still unsafe people to be around. Forgiveness sets us free for God to complete His work in us.

Forgiveness also has many levels; we can forgive from our head by an act of our will, but, we must also forgive from our hearts. The bible tells us if we do not forgive from our hearts, we will be turned over to the tormentors.

It can take a season of time for forgiveness to fully work inside our hearts. Within the heart is where the seventy times seven part of forgiveness takes place. This is spoken about in scriptures in Matthew 18.

**Matthew 18:21-22**

*21 Then Peter came to Him and said, "Lord, how often shall my brother sin against me and I forgive him? Up to seven times?" 22 Jesus said to him, "I do not say to you, up to seven times, but up to seventy times seven."*

Every time we see or think of the person and offence, it is another opportunity to forgive and release them. As we release them, we are being fully released ourselves. We will know we have truly forgiven from our hearts when we meet or think of the person without experiencing the anger, pain, or disappointment of the offence. We have moved into a place of true forgiveness. Once in that place we can finally pray for the person with a pure heart. We can then ask God to move in their life and heal them from the pain that caused them to offend or hurt us in the first place.

After John heard the counsellor's description of forgiveness, he knew that he was able to take this first step to be set free from the chains that had encased his heart for so long. He spoke the words and did not feel any emotion at all. But this was not a matter of feeling, but a matter of obeying what God asked him to do in His Word.

The counsellor also told him that he needed to forgive not only the abuser, Mr. Hanes, but also those that he felt did not protect him such as his parents and God. He also needed to forgive subsequent abusers like Phillip and the other men he had been in relationship with.

John also needed to extend forgiveness to the Psychologists that had not believed him nor helped him resolve the pain inside. The counsellor next explained that John had to forgive himself where he blamed himself because of the comfort and enjoyment he experienced in the sin.

Continuing on, the counsellor explained to John that he was not only tied to the people who had abused him, but he was also attached to the places where the abuse had taken place.

In scripture there are many references to the land needing to be cleansed from sins committed on it. For example:

**Numbers 35:33-34**

"*³³ So you shall not pollute the land where you are; for <u>blood defiles the land</u>, and no atonement can be made for the land, for the blood that is shed on it, except by the blood of him who shed it. ³⁴ Therefore <u>do not defile the land</u> which you inhabit, in the midst of which I dwell; for I the LORD dwell among the children of Israel."*

The book of **Leviticus, chapter 18**, contains a list of <u>sexual sins which defiles the land</u>, so the indication is that land needs cleansing from this defilement. For example look at **Verse 25**

"*²⁵ For the land is defiled; therefore I visit the punishment of its iniquity upon it, and the land vomits out its inhabitants."*

John knew that he often had flashbacks of the garage next door, and during that time he had experienced a stabbing pain in his heart and a feeling of panic.

It finally became clear to John that he had stuffed all that pain way down inside his heart, but at certain times when he was in a similar environment he felt panic, the same type of panic experienced the first time Mr. Hanes betrayed him.

John asked the counsellor to lead him in a prayer to break all ties to the people and places he was attached to in an ungodly way; and also the land where he had been defiled. After the prayer he felt as if a 100 pound weight had been lifted from his heart.

Next the counsellor told him that because of the lies he had believed about himself, others, and God, he had given the enemy a legal right to sit on a throne in the part of his heart that had been wounded through the abuse.

She drew him a diagram of what had happened. Drawing a valentine shaped heart on a sheet of paper; she then drew a circle inside it. Next, she drew a throne within the circle and put the number 5 next to the throne. (See page 26)

She then asked John how old he was when he had his first born again experience. He told her he had been 25 years old, shortly after meeting Joan. She wrote 25 in the other part of the heart outside the circle.

She went on to tell John that when he invited Jesus into his heart, Jesus did indeed come in and filled every part of his heart that He was able to. Unfortunately, because of the wounding, the enemy had carved out a well inside John's heart and was sitting enthroned on the lies he believed; as well as the resulting judgments and vows he had made of others and God, plus the core identities about himself.

The vow that John had made, *to hide and protect himself,* was like a brick wall around that part of his heart; and through each subsequent wound the wall had grown stronger and higher. John was unable to tear down this wall himself. He needed God to come inside and help him dismantle, not only the wall, but the stronghold that the enemy was hiding in. He needed God to do the work in him and for him.

Through the lies he had believed, John was virtually a prisoner inside his own heart, by his agreement with the enemy. Scriptures tells us there is power in agreement, so John had empowered the enemy through believing lies.

**Matthew 18:18-19**

*"18 Assuredly, I say to you, whatever you bind on earth will be bound in heaven, and whatever you loose on earth will be loosed in heaven. 19 Again I say to you <u>that if two of you agree on earth concerning anything</u> that they ask, <u>it will be done</u> for them by My Father in heaven."*

The protective cover over the well in John's heart was **control** in the form of **self-protection**, and it was held securely by the padlock of **shame** and **fear**.

The keys needed to open this lock were <u>Submission, Confession, and Repentance</u>. As John broke agreement with the lies, judgments, and vows he had made, he had to submit his will to God, and trust Him to dethrone the enemy,

| | |
|---|---|
| **Lies** | I am unworthy, my father rejected me |
| **Judgments** | Authorities will reject and/or abuse me |
| **Core Identities** | I am gay, I am betrayed, I am dirty and disgusting, and I am a victim |

| | |
|---|---|
| **Vows** | I will never trust anyone, I have to protect myself |
| **Ungodly Ties** | Father, Mother, Mr. Hanes, Phillip, others he had been involved with |
| **Attachments** | Garage, scout tent, etc. |
| **Strongholds** | Abandonment, Fear, Shame, Sexual sins |

John was exhausted and felt like quitting, but knew he was too close to freedom and deliverance to stop, so he asked the counsellor to help him pray.

When John left the counsellor's office that day he felt free of the burdens and fear he had carried most of his life. He knew in his heart the best was yet to come in his life and marriage.

## Chapter Five

# Rebecca – Voiceless & Unheard

Rebecca was amazed as the truth dawned on her that she was finally free from the awful pit she had spent most of her life hidden inside of. Fear and shame had been the hallmark of her family.

As a child she had watched in pain as her brothers and sisters had continually struggled to express the emotions which Rebecca knew they had bottled up inside. In her family there were several unwritten codes of conduct. Nobody had ever outlined or defined them, but you knew they were there because of the punishment that followed breaking the rules.

One of those rules was *"children were to be seen and not heard."* Rebecca therefore knew no matter how hard she tried to express her needs, she was not listened to. She did not remember the exact moment that she decided it was better to shut down and live inside her own head; but she must have, because that is what she had done.

Rebecca also remembered watching her brother as a young man struggling to express himself to their mother, and she felt his pain and frustration when his fears were not understood or acknowledged. The code of conduct that day told her *"It is not safe to express your emotions; and men are not supposed to cry."*

She had faint memories of being cuddled as a child and could still smell the scent of Old Spice as she sat on her dad's knee. She does not know when the cuddling stopped, but at some point, the family code of conduct dictated that *"You are grown up now and don't need to be cuddled when you get hurt, you are old enough to take care of yourself, just suck it up!"*

There were other 'codes of conduct' in her family but these three were the ones that impacted Rebecca the most in her life; the ones that helped her form the prison she had lived in up until today.

Because of the code of conduct learned in her family, she lived by these rules in most of her relationships during her teen and adult years. She had juggled and kept all parts of her life together, until the day her husband walked out on her and their children. She had never seen it coming because she was so busy doing the right thing and living by the rules.

The morning her husband left, Rebecca retreated to her safe place, and it took her five years to resurface. It took another five years to get the psychological and spiritual help she needed to piece together the puzzle of her life. Her father had been a large, gentle man who said very little. She could always trust her dad to be there in body, but he was passive and never confronted her mother or her abuse. So Rebecca did not expect a lot of input from the men in her life.

Her mother was a tired and angry woman, and Rebecca had seven siblings that kept her mom busy. As a child, Rebecca learned early not to bother her mom with things because she was either ignored, or received an angry or frustrated response. There was never an abundance of anything due to the expenses of running a household of ten. Rebecca's first memory of having a new dress was when she turned twelve. She had worn cast offs from her older sisters and had suffered ridicule as a result from her classmates in school. Consequently, Rebecca became very conscious of how she looked as a teenager, and it became a problem later when, as an adult, she filled her closets with clothes, most of which she never wore. Her husband had always complained, because of her abundance of clothes, he did not have room to hang his three pairs of pants in their bedroom closet.

As Marion, the counsellor, helped Rebecca unpack her life, she succeeded in getting rid of seventy-five percent of the clothes in her closet and the stuff in her home. As Rebecca became more comfortable in her own skin, her

## Rebecca – Voiceless and Unheard

home became more uncluttered and inviting to others.

Rebecca's main problem was that she had never felt safe or protected. With Marion's help, she had discovered that her dad's passivity had caused her to believe she was not protected by him from her mother. In one of her counselling sessions, she had a memory of running to show her mom a Popsicle stick basket she had made in school, and being ignored, because mom was busy making supper.

Rebecca had taken the basket outside, broke it into pieces, and buried it in the back yard. With it she had buried part of herself. She had buried the hope of ever being able to please others with an expression of her heart.

That day, Rebecca began to believe certain lies about herself and others that impacted the rest of her life. Until that day, she believed the following:

- ✓ What I do is not good enough for others to notice.
- ✓ I take second place with others to whatever is happening or what they are doing.
- ✓ I have no voice and others ignore me or don't see me or what I do.
- ✓ I don't have the right to celebrate or advertise what I do well.

Examining the patterns and cycles in her life; she saw that these beliefs had tormented her for the last 30 years. As a result, not only had she judged herself, but others and their

## Prisoner inside My Heart

expected response to her. The prison that she had dug for herself was called Disappointment, Fear, Shame, and Control. The first wall of her prison was called Shame. Shame is the sense of somehow we are flawed and nothing we do can ever make us acceptable. Another wall of her prison was fear, fear of not being accepted, and fear of never being good enough. Fear is an expectancy of something bad going to happen. Fear is a place between not knowing and knowing.

Another wall of her prison was control, and that is what she did the day she buried her school project. She had determined in her heart that day, "*if I can't please others I will please myself.*" The final wall of her prison was disappointment. She expected people to disappoint her because that was all she had known in her life up to this moment.

Marion asked Rebecca if she was ready to invite Jesus inside the prison she had built in order to destroy the stronghold inside her heart. Marion had explained that although Rebecca had invited Jesus into her heart as a fourteen year old girl, Jesus was never able to come into that place where the enemy had already established his own residence; inside of Rebecca's false belief systems.

Marion went on to tell her that only Jesus could expose and kick out the enemy, but He needed her permission to do so. So Rebecca proceeded to invite Jesus inside that walled off part of her heart, to begin the healing process.

The following is the model used by Marion to uncover Rebecca's false belief systems, her false identities, vows and judgments as a result of the wounding.

Rebecca asked God to show her the first time in her life she had the feeling that she was not important. He showed her the incident with her mother with Rebecca burying the basket in the back yard.

God proceeded to disclose the lies she believed as a result, and the subsequent vow that she had made to withdraw and protect herself. She had also vowed to comfort and celebrate herself, as no one else would ever do that for her.

The following is how Rebecca discovered the truth about herself that day.

# Ministry Model

**Marion**: "Rebecca, ask Jesus when was the first time that you felt that you were not important."

**Rebecca**: "I remember the day that my mother was too busy to look at my school project."

**Marion:** "What happened that day?"

**Rebecca:** "My teacher had all my classmates make baskets for their moms for Mother's Day. We took them home on the Friday, just before Mother's Day as a gift for our moms. I took mine home and gave it to my mom, but she was too busy to pay attention, so I tore it up and buried it in the backyard."

**Marion:** "How did you feel, as you were burying your basket that you had worked so hard to make?"

**Rebecca:** "I felt that I was not loved or appreciated. What I did was not important, and I was not important."

**Marion:** "What did you believe about others that day?"

**Rebecca:** "Others are only interested in themselves and what they are doing. They really don't care about me."

**Marion:** "What did you believe about God that day?"

**Rebecca:** "God was there, but He was just watching, He didn't stop it from happening. He doesn't care about me either."

**Marion:** "If others and God do not care about you Rebecca, What do you have to do?"

**Rebecca:** "I have to shut them out and protect myself, because apparently, no one else is going to."

**Marion:** "Is there anything else you chose to do that day?"

# Rebecca – Voiceless and Unheard

**Rebecca:** "I hid and comforted myself by wrapping myself in a big blanket and going to sleep."

**Marion:** "So Rebecca, let's examine the lies, judgments, and vows that you made that day."

As Marion and Rebecca discussed and isolated the lies, judgments and vows of that day, they discovered the false identities that Rebecca believed. Rebecca's core identity had been scarred and she believed the following about herself.

- ✓ I am unimportant
- ✓ I am unloved
- ✓ I am unheard
- ✓ I am unseen
- ✓ I am unnoticed
- ✓ I am not celebrated
- ✓ I am voiceless
- ✓ I am second
- ✓ I am not good enough
- ✓ I am fearful
- ✓ I am shameful
- ✓ I am hidden
- ✓ I am uncomforted

Rebecca had also made a **vow** that day. She vowed she would **hide, protect and comfort** herself. That vow became the wall around her heart which kept her from truly being intimate with others and herself.

**To summarize the lies Rebecca believed:**

- "What I do is not good enough for others to notice."
- "I take second place with others to whatever is happening or what they are doing."
- "I have no voice and others ignore me or don't see me or what I do."
- "I don't have the right to celebrate or advertise what I do well."

So with Marion's help, Rebecca began the process of breaking the agreements she had made with the enemy, and also the power of the judgments she had made of others and herself.

Rebecca did a half-skip as she walked towards her car that afternoon after leaving Marion's office. She felt joyful and light-hearted for the first time in a long, long time. She was happy that truth had been revealed and she looked forward to her next visit with the counsellor to achieve as much healing as possible from the wounds of the past.

## Chapter Six

# Carolyn. – Disappointment with God

Carolyn struggled to climb out of the hiding place called sleep which she often found herself in during these past few years. As she came to full consciousness, she also became aware of the pain in her heart. Once again she gave in to the dark feelings of hopelessness that has been her constant companion since the death of her only child, David. Her son David had only been three years old when the doctor discovered the tumor growing inside his brain. He had finally succumbed after two years of battling the disease.

The day Carolyn buried her baby; she had also buried a large part of her own heart. The pain in the pit of her stomach had never gone away since the first day she had heard the news of David's disease from the doctor. Five years had slipped by since the cold October day when Carolyn left her baby in the graveyard. One black day melted into another and any joy or zeal for life disappeared into a whirlpool of depression.

John-Marc, Carolyn's husband, had given up trying to initiate social events and inviting friends or family into their home. Carolyn was never able to muster enough strength to be up for it, or to interact at these functions. She was eternally tired and every muscle and joint in her body ached. It seemed to fight her when she aimlessly wandered through her home trying to do the little bits of housekeeping left over by the housekeeper. John-Marc had hired Anna to help Carolyn when David was battling the disease and Carolyn had to be in and out of the hospital with him.

That morning as Carolyn turned over in bed she saw John-Marc's shirt, that he had worn yesterday, thrown across the chest at the foot of the bed. She reached out and grabbed it burying her face, as tears stung her eyes. She was remembering the words he had spoken last night just before he left to go sleep in the spare bedroom once again.

As she recognized John-Marc's scent from his shirt; his parting words came back to pierce her heart like a sword. The words he shot at her while leaving the room had jolted her out of her own self-pity. "Carolyn just remember, you may have lost your son, but I lost my son and wife at the same time." He went on to say; "Things will have to change around here because I cannot go on living my life this way."

## Carolyn — Disappointment With God

Carolyn's mind went back to when she had first met John-Marc, and how much they had respected and loved each other. They had spent hours planning not only their marriage, but their life together, how many children they would have, and even what they wanted to do with grandchildren when they came.

"Oh God", Carolyn cried out, "What happened to me, where did I go."

"You ran away from me and hid, Carolyn." The voice seemed to come from all four corners of the room at once. "You are angry at me because you blamed me for not healing your son." The voice became silent.

Carolyn knew God's voice; she knew her heavenly Father has just spoken to her and sliced open all the self-protective walls she had erected. Her soul lay bare before her maker. Instead of running into God when she lost her David, she had blamed God and ran away from Him. How was she going to find her way back home to Father God?

The first commandment was like a neon light inside of Carolyn's mind. On and off blinked the words "You shall have no other gods before Me." As Carolyn mulled over these words, it became clear that she had placed David, God's creation and gift to her, above The Creator Himself. She knew that any person, position or thing that she placed ahead of God became Idolatry, and she had done that with

David. It had taken three years of trying before she had become pregnant with David, and from the moment of his birth, he was the center of her world.

She looked back and saw how she had put God on hold as the chores of new motherhood took over. Next the disease and battling it became the center of her existence. Oh yes, she had called on God to help, but slowly as the disease took over, she gave up on God; and settled into disappointment with Him, as death claimed her baby.

As she was thinking about these things, she realized that she needed some help to unravel what God had shown her. She made an appointment to see Valerie, the counsellor on staff at her church

During her first visit with Valerie, the issue of Carolyn's disappointment with God was identified. Carolyn was surprised to find out that Valerie did not stop at her unveiling the current disappointment, but wanted to track it back to its roots. She used the example that if we have an apple tree growing in our back yard and want to get rid of the apples, merely cutting the tree down will not work. She said within a few years you would have a new crop of fruit because the tree would grow again if the roots were not dug up and removed.

Valerie asked Carolyn if she would give God permission to show her the first time in her life she was

## Carolyn — Disappointment With God

disappointed with Him.

Immediately she remembered when she was seven years old, her dog Toby got sick and she prayed that God would heal him. Toby eventually died and Carolyn was so angry with God that she refused to go to Sunday school, and would not even pray when her mom tucked her in at night.

God showed Carolyn that on the day Toby died, she had believed *'She could not trust God with the ones she loved most.'* She had closed part of her heart towards God that day, and had forgotten all about it, until He reminded her. But the enemy had never forgotten, and knew the wound was inside her, and he could use it to torment her and destroy her trust in God.

Valerie led her in a prayer of repentance for her judgment and disappointment with God. Then they settled in to dismantle the stronghold the enemy has erected inside Carolyn's heart.

(See Route to Freedom at the end of this book to work through your own stronghold of disappointment with God).

## Prayer to confess Disappointment and Anger towards God.

*Father God, I confess that I have been angry with You and judged You. I believed that You disappointed me by not being there when I felt I needed You the most. Therefore, I judged You as being untrustworthy. I know that You are faithful in all your ways; therefore, I repent for my anger and for closing my heart to you. I choose to stop blaming You and place the blame where it belongs, on the enemy, others, and myself. I declare that you are a faithful God and you will be faithful to me. Lord please forgive me, come in and heal my wounded heart and set me free. I pray this in The Name of Jesus Christ, My Lord. Amen!*

# Chapter Seven

## Jim & Joanne - Marriage on the Rocks

Jim and Joanne sat in the Therapist's office as far away from each other as they could get and still be seated on the same sofa. Their body language spoke separation, with their legs crossed and facing away from each other, while their arms formed barriers to protect their hearts. They had sought counsel because their marriage was in serious trouble. If something did not happen soon, divorce seemed to be their only way out of the pain. They did not speak to each other, but instead to the marriage therapist thereby, completely avoiding looking in each other's direction.

Sam, the marriage therapist, started with the usual list of questions he used with new couples.

"Well Joanne, ladies first, tell me what you see as the core reason you both have sought counsel for your marriage?"

"I cannot find the words to tell you what is happening Sam, only what I feel," Joanne replied.

"So tell me your feelings Joanne," Sam encouraged her.

"I feel Jim is busy living his own life and I am just an appendage. Jim is always doing his own thing and leaves family matters to me. If he is not going out to golf or a ball game, he is usually in his office on his computer, not wanting to be disturbed. Our children are growing up fatherless, even with a father in the house." Joanne did not seem to take a breath as all these statements tumbled out of her one after another.

"Thank you Joanne," Sam said as he turned his attention to Jim.

"Jim how do you perceive what is happening within your marriage?"

"I think Joanne lives too much out of her feelings to begin with, and what I really think is that she does not know how to be a good wife. She does not respect me the way my father was respected by my mother."

"So what I am hearing Jim, is that you do not feel respected by your wife." Jim nodded. "Tell me Jim," Sam continued, "what is your definition of respect?" Jim looked at Sam in a puzzled way and then proceeded to give him a definition of what he felt respect looked like.

Sam summarized what Jim had told him when he had finished. "So Jim, you see respect as having a completely compliant wife who does whatever you want without question or opinion of her own, just like your mom."

"Hey Sam, when you put it like that you make me out to be a controlling monster, just like my father." Jim's eyes widened as the penny dropped and he fully saw himself for the first time.

He had judged his father and mother growing up and now he was living out that judgment in his own life. "Okay Sam, I see what has happened but what can we do to fix the mess we are in?" Jim asked.

Sam replied to both of them; "Well we need to look at your family environment while growing up, as well as Joanne's to see how each of your belief systems has allowed this situation to develop within your marriage."

"I also need to know that both of you are willing to stick out the process of digging up the stuff from the past that created the relationship you have with each other today." "This process may cause pain for each of you as you examine your own part in helping to forge the interactions that go on within your marriage."

"Anything is better than what is happening with us now," Jim replied.

"I am in this for the long haul," Joanne told Sam, as she uncrossed her arm and sat back in her seat.

Over the next few visits, with the help of homework sheets, given to them by Sam, the couple was able to find some root issues in their lives highlighting why they behaved towards each other the way they did.

But the greater healing for Jim and Joanne came in the individual sessions as Sam dealt with their own personal wounds. These wounds caused them to react to each other through coping mechanisms formed during their childhood.

Joanne's father was a travelling salesman and was away for extended periods of time. Her mother had done what was necessary to keep the house running, and raise her girls the best way she could without a father there to help. Her mom was a self-sufficient woman who was able to fix most things around the house including the broken faucets, repair of electrical break-downs, and other household problems. She even learned to handle a chain-saw to cut the wood that was needed for the fireplace. Joanne and her sister Maria had learned and modeled their mother's independence, while Ellie, the youngest had been the prissy one and refused to do man's work as she called it.

Joanne and Maria had often judged and joked about the boys in their age group who could not do any manual labour. They had considered them to be unmanly.

## Jim & Joanne — Marriage on the Rocks

When Joanne met and married Jim, he was a real handy man and that intrigued her and made her feel protected when he would take a tool from her and say "*let me do that for you.*"

Over the years though, as Jim got busier at work. Joanne never bothered him with the little things that needed fixing, she just did it herself because after all, she was capable.

As the years passed, she resented Jim for leaving all the work up to her. She had shut her heart towards Jim and avoided his attempts at affection.

As Sam led Joanne through ministry, they discovered her anger at Jim was really displaced anger at her father. Joanne had watched her mother struggle under the load of running the home, caring for Joanne and her sisters, as well as working part time to supplement the family income. She had grown to judge and disrespect her father because he was absent and non-supportive of her mother.

She had judged him as inadequate as a father and husband. She had also judged her mother as being a victim and made a vow to never be like her mother or marry a man like her father.

As she examined her life, she became aware that she was living a life just like her mother's, and Jim was acting like her dad by being emotionally absent even while at home.

Jim has also judged his parents. He had judged his dad as being bossy and demanding. He had judged his mother as escaping family involvement through her woman's group participation and crafts.

He had also judged Joanne of being bossy and demanding, just like his dad, because she was always nagging him about spending more time with her and the kids.

Sam showed Jim how he had programmed his wife to be like his dad by neglecting his duty as a father and keeping busy with his own interests, just as his mom had done. Because of Joanne's abandonment issues with her father she was being triggered continually by his non-participation in family relationship. The judgments, lies, and fears were causing the miscommunication and marital problems between Joanne and Jim.

When they had a joint session with Sam, they were able to discuss and learn how to stop pushing each other's buttons. They also learned to quickly ask each other for forgiveness if they failed, instead of isolating or becoming independent.

No marriage relationship is perfect, but open communication and understanding can go a long way in building bridges where previously there were fences caused by defenses due to offences taken.

If you are experiencing marital problems, get healing for yourself first, before insisting that your partner gets fixed. By receiving healing for your own wounds, using the Route to Freedom at the end of this book, you can do what is necessary to help heal your marriage where you have caused pain for your partner.

## Chapter Eight

# Rose – The Victim

Rose stood angry and confused with the broken handle of the broom in her hands. She had just broken it over her knee and had threatened her mother that if she hit her once again, she would hit back. Her mother had just used the same broom to beat Rose because her job of cleaning the kitchen floor was not good enough to please her mother. Rose had washed the floor on her hands and knees because according to her mother, that was the only correct way to wash a floor.

Rose was fourteen years old, and had withstood many harsh words and beatings from the hands of her mother. Her words to her mother that day were *"I will kill you if you ever touch me again."* Her mother backed away and never laid a hand on her again, but harsh words were the whip her mom continued to use to keep Rose under her control.

## Rose — The Victim

Rose grew up in a large family and being one of the youngest, she was bossed around by her older siblings. They often got her to do things they knew would get them into trouble if they were caught. She remembers the day her two older sisters urged her to go inside the school and steal money from a purse hanging on a coat rack in the hallway. She was only eight years old at the time, and was caught and severely punished by the girl who owned the purse. She took the blame that day and was labeled a "little thief," and that label stayed in her mind for years. She was always afraid that she would be blamed if something went missing or got lost.

These two incidents, and other similar painful experiences of childhood, caused Rose to grow up believing that there was something wrong with her. She felt that she could not trust those in authority over her to protect her. She also believed authority figures would abuse her and treat her harshly, and that she could not trust them to have her best interests at heart.

Her heart had also determined that if she was going to be safe in this world, she would have to learn to protect herself in order to survive. She became a people pleaser in her young adult years, but always kept her heart shielded from those she associated it. She was a master at reading people and anticipating their needs, so she was well received within the circles that she moved in.

Her fear of being deceived by those closest to her, kept her out of a lot of trouble in her late teens and young adult life. She therefore missed the drug and free sex of the Hippie era she grew up in.

She would have lived her entire life in fear, had she not sought the help of a counsellor because of some relational problems she was experiencing. Rose had been victimized her entire life by the control of predators who had preyed on her vulnerability and good will. Her mother had used intimidation and fear of punishment, while her sisters had used manipulation and coercion to get her to do what they wanted.

Because Rose was young when she was abused, she was primed as a victim for other predator spirits in her environment to abuse her. As a young girl she was molested by a neighbour and that left her feeling full of guilt and shame.

Examining her experiences; Rose and the counsellor mapped out the patterns and cycles of her life that led her to believe certain things about herself and others.

**The lies that Rose had believed were:**

- ✓ I cannot trust those closest to me to protect me nor have my best interests at heart.

- Others will manipulate me to fulfill their needs and leave me to be punished for it.
- If I do not do what others want, they will punish me by withholding their love or abuse me.
- No matter how hard I try, my efforts are never good enough to please others.
- I am second best at what I do, others can do the task better, and my best is not enough.
- God put me into this world to be controlled by others and their needs.
- Others profit from my effort and pain.

She had also made some vows and judgments that kept her from being real with herself, others and God.

**She had vowed:**
- I will never fully trust anyone in authority.
- I will protect myself so others will not use and abuse me.

**She had also made the following judgments:**
- God did not protect me; He put me in a family that abused me.
- You cannot trust others to have your best interests at heart.

- ✓ Authority will use you for your talents and gifting and then throw you away.

From these lies, judgments, and vows the counsellor showed Rose that she had assumed and lived a false identity.

Some of the false identities she had assumed were:

- ✓ I am abused
- ✓ I am alone
- ✓ I am controlled
- ✓ I am unprotected
- ✓ I am mistrusted
- ✓ I am my own protector
- ✓ I am manipulated
- ✓ I am trapped
- ✓ I am angry
- ✓ I am a victim

Rose learned from her counsellor that when we have been victims of others and their control, we learn to control others ourselves. This causes us to develop many coping mechanisms to prevent being victims of controlling people. Our main objective is to keep from being hurt by the predator spirit of the controller.

We will either reject or rebel against the person

## Rose — The Victim

attempting to control us, and we can do this passively or aggressively. If we sense that someone is a predator, we will confront them or isolate from them, depending on our level of self confidence or insecurities. When we are strong in our sense of self worth, we usually have correct boundaries and will not allow others to manipulate us in any way.

She also learned from her counsellor that this same victim/predator relationship happens when people are taken captive by others, such as in hostage taking, cults, prisoners of war, kidnapping, etc. The person with a predator spirit is one who has most likely once been a victim themselves. Rose was surprised as the counsellor showed her where she had been a predator because of her desire to protect herself from hurt.

Predator is a harsh word and made Rose think of wolves stalking deer, cats hunting mice, or rapists taking advantage of innocent children. She shuttered as the counsellor showed her how her manipulation of others was really predator based when she took advantage of those who were weaker than, or not as informed as she was.

Rose knew that God was not pleased with her actions and was quick to repent of her past participation and attitudes in this area. Slowly the counsellor unraveled the way the enemy had taken Rose captive by the actions of others in her life when she was a child.

Through the lies, judgments, vows, and wrong labels she had received, the enemy created a stronghold in which he had made himself secure. He had built a fortress in her heart, and she was the watchman guarding the stronghold through her self-protection and vows not to trust anyone.

Rose was not able to escape the stronghold by herself, nor could the counsellor do it for her through her learned techniques in counselling or ministry. Only the power of God could invade the fortress which had imprisoned her all these years. The only thing that Rose could do was invite God to come into her self-made fortress, and kick the enemy out. The prison had to be dismantled from the inside out.

Rose started by confessing to God her rebellion and self-protection by not trusting Him to protect her. She next invited Him to come in and do the work in and for her, that she could not do herself. She then broke her agreement with the lies that she believed about herself, others and God.

She next broke the <u>agreement</u> with the judgments, vows and false labels she had assumed. She broke the power of the judgments and vows and asked God to stop all the sowing and reaping cycles that had happened as a result.

Next she resigned as being her own Saviour. The counsellor showed her that when she had assumed the "I am" labels; she not only judged herself, but she had kicked Jesus off the throne of her heart as The Great "I AM". There is

# Rose – The Victim

only one "I AM" and that is the God of Israel. When we believe lies about our identity, that are contrary to God's Word, we enthrone ourselves as our own god. Rose decided to find out her true identity according to the Word of God, and His opinion of who she is, not the opinion of others or herself.

| **False "I AM"** | **True "I AM"** |
| --- | --- |
| I am abused | I am healed |
| I am alone | I am never alone |
| I am controlled | I am free to be me |
| I am unprotected | I am protected by God |
| I am mistrusted | I am trustworthy |
| I am my own protector | I am protected by God |
| I am manipulated | I am free to move and think |
| I am trapped | I am released |
| I am angry | I am at peace |
| I am a victim | I am an over-Comer |

After establishing her true identity, Rose dealt with the lies she has lived her life through. It was as if she had put on tinted glasses, and thereafter saw life in a different way because of the lies she had come into agreement with. Working with the counsellor, they examined each lie individually and found out the truth with the help of the Holy Spirit.

The first lie that she had to deal with was: *"I cannot trust those closest to me to protect me or have my best interests at heart."*

She confessed her sin of making a covenant with the enemy by believing the lie and opening the door for him to create a stronghold in her heart.

She repented and asked God to forgive her for aligning herself with the devil and rebelling against God. She next forgave her ancestors who had opened the door to abuse and rebellion within the family bloodline.

The counsellor led her through forgiving her mother and sisters, as well as her father because he did not protect her from her mother.

Rose went on to forgive others in her life whom she felt had not taken care of her. She forgave old boyfriends, schoolmates, close friends, her husband, and teachers, everyone that the Holy Spirit brought to her mind.

Once she forgave them; she broke ungodly attachments to these people because of unmet needs and expectations. She also broke ungodly attachments to the places of offence. She asked God to remove the imprint of the people from her body, soul and spirit.

The counsellor next asked God to take the captive part of Rose that the enemy had imprisoned, and seat it in heavenly places in Christ Jesus according to Ephesians.

**Ephesians 1:20**

"Which He worked **in** Christ when He raised Him from the dead and **seated Him** at His right hand **in** the **heavenly places**,"

**Ephesians 2:6**

"And **raised us up together, and made us sit together in** the **heavenly places** in Christ Jesus,"

From that place of immunity, she asked God to tell Rose the truth.

In her spirit Rose heard His strong voice of reassurance as God told her that His original plan for all His children was a loving and caring home to fashion His children for reigning. The enemy had circumvented his plan in the Garden of Eden and used the blame, shame and tame tactic on His creation.

Since Adam and Eve there had been abuse and blame-shifting within families. Rose's parents were the result of the fall, just like all others, and there were no perfect families on earth.

Her mother was operating out of her own unhealed issues and had hurt Rose as a result.

He went on to tell her that there were trustworthy people, and He had, and would continue to send them into her life. He said that He had given her a keen sense of discernment, and when she sought the direction of The Holy

Spirit, she would know whom to trust. He also told her that He was going to bring other people into her life that would show her uncommon favour. Rose thanked the Lord for His love and the counsellor read back to her what she had scribed as Rose heard from God.

They went on to deal with each lie individually, and finally Rose felt as if she had been released out of a prison and was now where she knew she truly belonged, hidden in Christ. From that place she knew she did not have to defend herself any longer. God was her defense and she felt fully and truly safe for the first time in her life.

## Chapter Nine

# Dianne – Aborted Hope

It took all of Dianne's strength to smile at the doctor as she said goodbye and left his office that afternoon. All her expectations and hopes had rolled up into a little ball and crashed to the bottom of her stomach like a lead weight. Once again her dreams had been dashed to pieces with the words of the doctor, "Not this month Dianne." Gerry and Dianne had been married now for 10 years and every month, her desire for a baby peaked into longing only to be flung to the ground as quickly as a roller coaster plunging from the highest tower at the fairgrounds.

Every month she wrestled with anger, shame, fear, and guilt blaming herself once again for the abortion she had when she was seventeen.

As Dianne parked her car in the garage and

went into her home, she dreaded the question that Gerry always asked at this time of the month. Gerry came from a large loving family and longed for his own children, so he could leave his own legacy.

Their big modern home sounded hollow as Diane walked down the hallway towards the kitchen; as hollow as her heart felt right now. What was the purpose of all this space and these lovely possessions, if she didn't have a child to fill the aching in her heart?

She steeled herself emotionally and automatically started to prepare dinner. She had purchased a pre-packaged lasagna on the way home, which she popped into the oven and started on the salad and dessert. Gerry had invited Elise and Morgan, a new couple from church, for a meal, so she took extra care in setting the table, arranging some candles and flowers to brighten up the room.

The doctor's afternoon news did not cross her mind again until she was removing the dishes from the table to bring out coffee and dessert. Elise followed her into the kitchen with some dishes and chatted away as they prepared the coffee. Elise surprised her with the question, *"Are you planning on having children?"* Dianne could no longer hold back her tears and turned and quickly went into the guest bathroom. She stayed in there long enough to gain composure and then went back into the kitchen.

Elise apologized for upsetting her and went on to tell

her about how she also experienced a difficult time conceiving. She said she had gone to a grief counsellor to help her deal with some unresolved issues. It had been a fruitful experience for her and she received healing for some past wounds, and six months later she was pregnant with her first child. "If you would like Dianne, I can give you her contact information," Elise offered. Dianne agreed as they headed back into the dining room with the coffee for their husbands.

Three weeks later Dianne found herself seated in a comfortable chair across from Sandra, a Psychotherapist who specialized in grief counselling. As Sandra drew Dianne out with carefully worded statements and questions, Dianne warmed up to the woman. About twenty minutes later, Sandra gave a summary of what she had gleaned from Dianne in their initial interview.

"Dianne," she said, "you seem to be depressed by the fact that you have not been able to carry a child full term. You told me you have miscarried one child and possibly another, as you had missed two menstrual cycles. So there may be a possibility that you have lost 2 babies since attempting to become pregnant."

"Tell me Dianne, how does it make you feel when you think about the possibility of losing 2 children?"

Dianne responded by saying she felt angry and cheated, and she also felt sad and hopeless. Sandra next asked Dianne if she remembered other times in her life she experienced feeling this way.

Dianne said "no I do not remember anything". She said all she felt was numb and confused when she tried to think about when she first felt this way.

Sandra replied, "It sounds Dianne that you may have shut down your emotions at some point and now you cannot access them. This is called repression, but there is someone who knows exactly what the emotions are and when you shut them down."

"Who is that?" Dianne asked. "The Spirit of God, Sandra replied, He knows everything about us. Do you think you can trust God enough to allow him to reveal the source of those feelings?"

"Okay, Dianne said, but how do I do that?"

"Let me lead you in a prayer Dianne, all I need you to do is pay attention to what you are feeling in your heart, in your physical body and what is happening with your thoughts."

After Dianne gave her permission, Sandra led her in the following prayer:

## Dianne – Aborted Hope

"Dear Father God,

(**Note**: some people are more comfortable addressing Jesus or Holy Spirit)

*I ask you to reveal to me where and when I shut down my emotions. I invite you to come into my heart, past all my self-protective defenses and start to dismantle any strongholds within me. I give you permission to destroy all structures, supporting lies, judgments, and vows that I have made or believed. I know I cannot do this for myself, so I ask You to do it for me. I take authority over every other voice, be it my own inner voice or the voice of the enemy of my soul. I trust you Father to show me the truth now."*

Several minutes passed, and then tears started to form on Dianne's lashes.

Sandra then asked, "What are you seeing, feeling or remembering Dianne?"

"I was thinking of the day I aborted a baby when I was 17 years old."

"Tell me some more about what happened at that time Dianne?"

"I got drunk at a party when I was 17 and ended up sleeping with Barry, my boyfriend. As a result I became pregnant. I told Barry, when I knew for sure, but he completely rejected me. He said I wasn't going to hang it on him; and he even doubted that it was actually his. I was humiliated, Barry was the first boy I had been intimate with and he betrayed me completely."

"What did you feel or believe about yourself because of that incident, Dianne?"

Dianne replied, "I felt exposed, vulnerable, used and rejected. I also felt it was my fault for getting drunk and losing control. I felt I can never trust a man again because they will use and abuse, and then reject me."

"Where was God in this situation, Dianne?"

"I didn't know Him, the way I do today. I know He is always with me, but I guess I believed He could have prevented it from happening, but He didn't, so I closed my heart to Him.

I decided that I would take control and get rid of the problem; so, I had an abortion and never told anyone. It seemed the easy way out, and other girls at high school had done the same thing. Afterward, I felt guilty; I had murdered my own child. I felt I could never forgive myself and I was not worthy to have another child."

"Dianne, there seems to be a lot of judgments and vows you made of yourself, others, as well as God, through this wounding in your life."

"I never allowed myself to think about it for years, it was far too painful, I just stuffed it." Dianne said

"Shall we ask God what He wants to say to you about it now?" Sandra asked her.

"I am afraid He will condemn me," replied Dianne.

"Scriptures tell us that 'our sins may be as scarlet, but they shall be white as snow'", Sandra told her.

"God is showing me that what happened was not His best intention for me. I was a victim, and I ended up condemning myself and labeling myself as unworthy, because of what happened. He said that Barry was immature and rather than assume responsibility for his part in the situation, chose to put the blame on me and I had willingly assumed it. God says a real man protects a woman, even from herself. Because I hated myself for what I had done, I became my own accuser, and shut down my heart because it was too painful to feel. He wants to heal my heart if I will allow Him."

"Will you allow Him Dianne?" Sandra asked.

"Oh yes," Dianne replied.

"Are you able to forgive that 17 year old girl, Dianne, as well as Barry?" Sandra asked her.

"Yes," Dianne answered.

"Okay, let's break agreement with the lies, judgments and vows you made at that time." Sandra led her through confessing, repenting of, and renouncing the lies, judgments and vows.

Next, she broke all ungodly soul ties with Barry, as well as all ungodly attachments with the house where the incident happened. She went on to lead Dianne in a prayer to break all defilement off the land and time that it happened. She asked God to cleanse the land and time and to cleanse Dianne of all defilement.

She next broke her free from all the false Identities that Dianne had assumed because of the abortion.

**Dianne's False I am statements:**

| <u>False I AM</u> | <u>True I AM</u> |
|---|---|
| I am Shameful | I am the righteousness of God |
| I am exposed | I am covered by His Wings |
| I am vulnerable | I am protected by God |
| I am used | I am made whole |
| I am rejected | I am accepted in the Beloved |
| I am unworthy | I am made worthy through Christ |
| I am a murderer | I am justified by The Blood of Jesus Christ |
| I am guilty | I am forgiven |

Next she broke the power of the vow that she was not worthy of forgiveness or to have another child.

Dianne walked out of Sandra's office that day free from the guilt that she had carried on her shoulders for 20 years. She knew she was forgiven and fresh hope welled up within her as she got into her car and headed towards home.

## Chapter Ten

# Sonya – Sex Slave Survivor

Barbara pulled her car into the parking lot of her favorite take-out restaurant to pick up dinner for her family. The meeting she had attended went way later than expected, and now there was no time to prepare a meal for her hungry kids and husband. She parked the car next to a dumpster because it was the only space available because Scott's Chicken Villa was always packed on Fridays. As she stepped out of the car she saw a young girl bend down and crawl from behind the dumpster and hide in front of her car.

Barbara called out to her, "What are you doing there, is something wrong?"

"Please lady, help me, he's going to kill me if he catches me." the young girl replied.

## Dianne – Aborted Hope

"Who will kill you?" Barbara asked.

"Please help me, get me out of here, please." The look of terror in the young woman eyes pierced Barbara's heart.

Barbara still wonders what caused her to go against her own self-protective instincts and invite the young woman into her vehicle. For all she knew, the young girl could have been a mass murderer. But the desperation and fear on the young woman's face caused her mothering instincts to flip into place.

"Get in the car and down on the floor, I will get you out of here," Barbara told her. Slowly Barbara backed up her car and left the parking lot, watching carefully to see if anyone was following her. She drove down Main Street asking the young girl questions as they went.

"What is your name dear?" Barbara asked.

"Sonja", the girl replied.

"Who is trying to kill you Sonja?" Barbara asked.

"The man who forced me to have sex with all the men he brought to the house where I was being held against my will," Sonja told.her. The young girl started to cry with wrenching sobs, punctuated with sharp intakes of breath. Barbara noted that as Sonja cried her whole body had started to let go of the rigid vigilance she saw all over her when she first entered the car.

"Where is your home, and how did you get to Scott's Villa?" Barbara asked her softly. She noticed that the young girl spoke English with a heavy European accent.

Sonja replied, "I was born in Poland and moved to the United States with my parents 5 years ago. I did not have the necessary education to get a good job, so I replied to a newspaper advertisement in up-state New York to work as a nanny. After I was hired for the job, the woman who hired me suggested I give her my passport to put in her safe for protection. I trusted her and gave it to her. Three days later a man came to the house and they gave me a needle and the next thing I knew, I was in another house in another town, and a man named Ed raped me. From that day at least 6 months ago, I have been raped repeatedly by whatever man came into my room.

"I was kept in a large house and locked in a room and not allowed anywhere near a phone. I tried once and was beaten by Ed. He is the one I was hiding from when you found me." Sonja broke into sobs again and Barbara let her cry for a while as she steered her car through traffic.

"I begged them to let me go, but they would beat me and forced me to submit; what part of the United States am I in?" Sonya asked

"Honey, you are in Canada, in a city called Toronto which is in the province of Ontario. You are two hours north of the Canadian and US border," Barbara informed her.

"I don't understand, how did I get here?" Sonja asked.

"You were most likely smuggled across the US border, by this man called Ed," Barbara replied.

Barbara told Sonja that she was going to call her husband, who was a police officer, to meet her at police headquarters just 15 minutes drive away.

Sonja looked at her in fear, so Barbara comforted her and told her, she would stay with her until she knew she was absolutely safe. She used her cell phone to call Jim and explain what had happened and why she was so late for supper.

As they walked into the back door of the police station Barbara hugged Sonja's shoulders to reassure her.

Shirley, the station administrator on duty, ushered them into an office and closed the door behind her. "Jim called to say he is on the way and will be here any moment." Shirley told her. "In the meantime Barbara, Sergeant Daphne Mercer will be in to start taking a statement. Can I get you some water or a coffee while you are waiting?"

Sgt. Daphne was just starting to take Sonja's statement when Jim walked through the door. Barbara felt a load lift off her shoulders; she knew she could depend on Jim to do the right thing and protect everyone there. As Daphne continued to question Sonja; Barbara filled Jim in on what had happened at the Take-out parking lot. "What is going to happen to her once she gives her statement?" Barbara asked Jim.

"She will have to be kept in protective custody, until we can check out her statement, make arrests, and she will have to identify her captors. If what I suspect is happening, there is a prostitution ring with human trafficking happening right here in our neighborhood. There are probably other girls and maybe even guys who are virtual sex slaves in our city. If we do this right we can bust the whole thing wide open," Jim told Barbara.

"Will Sonja be safe Jim?" Barbara wanted to know.

"Yes dear, we have safe houses for situations like this. She will be taken there undercover and protected until the trial."

"Can I visit her there Jim? She needs someone to talk to about this whole thing."

"Barbara, we have social workers and counsellors that will be helping her, but if you want to visit her, I can arrange it. Let's go home to the kids; Marge from next door is watching them." Barbara took a few minutes to reassure Sonja that she was going to be looked after and protected. She told her she would come to see her in a few days, and then left for home.

As Barbara prepared for bed that evening she could not get Sonja out of her mind. Sonja was only 5 years older than her daughter and she shuttered at the thought of her young daughter being abused the way that Sonja had been. Life seemed so unfair at times. She decided that she would visit Sonja on Sunday afternoon, while her family was relaxing after church.

Jim had made arrangements as promised; and on Sunday, around three in the afternoon, Barbara headed to the address he had given her. Sonja was happy to see her and looked more relaxed and at peace than she had on the Friday evening.

The Greens, the family Sonja was staying with, must have bought her some clothes, because she had on new jeans and a sweater, as well as new runners. The Greens left them alone in the living room after serving coffee and a snack. Barbara inquired if Sonja was comfortable with her new location. "I am okay here, but I really want to go home and be with my mom and dad. I spoke to them last night, after Sgt. Daphne phoned to let them know where I was. My mom was crying on the phone, Dad and Mom have been so worried because they had not heard from me in 6 months.

The lady from the nanny job told them I had run away. They didn't know how to find me and didn't have enough money to pay anyone to help search for me. Mom wanted me to come home immediately, but she now understands that is impossible until the police release me to go."

Barbara said, "I am glad you made contact with your family, I know how devastated I would be if my daughter disappeared." Barbara went on to ask Sonja, how she was coping herself, with the abuse she had experienced over the past 6 months.

"I am angry at Ed and the people who hurt me, but sometimes I also get angry at myself for being taken advantage of and not trying to escape sooner. I feel dirty and used, I am ashamed of myself."

Barbara comforted her with the fact that she was a victim and needed to stop blaming herself because of what had happened to her. From their conversation, Barbara saw that Sonja would need some additional counselling besides what she would receive through the police. Her core identity had been attacked and she needed to know she was not to blame for what had happened to her. Barbara got permission from the police and arranged for Mary, the counsellor at church to meet with Sonja once a week.

Mary noted in her first session with Sonja that she had taken on a victim mentality, which was completely understandable. As she questioned the girl further, she came to realize that it was a mindset which Sonja had grown up with. Questioning her further, she found that her parents and grandparents had the same way of thinking.

The family history which Mary took from Sonja revealed Sonja's ancestors had suffered persecution in more than one way. They had been involved in two wars, as well as being forced to resettle in a new country; leaving them feeling that they were unwanted and rejected.

When Sonja's parents moved to the United States, They once again experienced the rejection and victimization known by their forefathers.

As Mary outlined the patterns of being a victim to Sonja, she showed her how her great grandparents, grandparents, parents and now Sonja had all been victimized by the environment and cultures of their day.

"How can we stop this Mary?" Sonja asked.

Sonja, who had been raised as an Orthodox Catholic, listened intently as Mary began to explain the message of salvation and the completed work of the Cross of Jesus Christ.

As Mary explained things to her, Sonja began to see and understand that Jesus was a real Savior, not just a figure on the cross as she had seen him previously. "In the bible, in

John 16:33, it tells us that we will have tribulation while we live in this world." Mary told her. "That word, tribulation, means we will have troubles and sorrows. It continues in that same verse to say that we can have joy in all circumstances because He, Jesus, has overcome the world."

"In some bibles, the words that Jesus spoke are written in red letters so we can know exactly what Jesus said to us while He was alive. There is an old expression that says: *'Read the **Red**, before bed and wake up with a clean heart and head.'* Sometimes it is intimidating to attempt to read the bible because it being such a long book, but if we read it a chapter at a time, it is much easier. So, from this scripture that I quoted to you Sonja, we shouldn't be surprised when trouble comes, but it is how we respond to the trial that determines our future. Our attitude determines our altitude, whether we rise or fall."

"Your abusers can, through your reactions, determine the outcome of your future. They stole 6 months of your life, but you get to decide if they will steal the rest of your life. You can stay in the place of being a victim, full of self pity and unforgiveness, locked to your captors through anger and bitterness; or you can cut yourself free by forgiving them. Yes, I know they are guilty and need to be punished for what they did to you and others, but God, Who is the greatest Judge of all times, gets to judge them, not you."

"When we won't forgive we take a fish hook and dig it

deeply into our own heart and give the string attached to it to the person who offended us. We are permanently attached to that person for life, unless we break the connection through forgiveness and release. Forgiveness is a choice and an act of our will. We may not feel the forgiveness at first, but when we continue to forgive the offenders, we come to a place of freedom where the offence no longer has power to hurt us.

I cannot explain to you how it happens or why it works, I just know that forgiveness is a principle of God's Word that does work, if we apply it."

As Mary led Sonja through forgiving her captors, she was also able to identify and break some further judgments and vows that Sonja had made of the abusers as well as herself. She also led her though a prayer of renouncing a victim mentality that had been in her generational bloodline for centuries. The following is the prayer that she prayed:

**PRAYER TO BREAK VICTIM AND PREDATOR SPIRIT**

*Father God of Abraham;*
*I repent on behalf of my ancestors and myself for the fear of man. I repent for submitting to a predator spirit in any person and giving them authority over me. I forgive every person who has used me as a victim. Jesus I give you the throne of my heart. I ask you to hide me in the Cross and sever every ungodly connection, (spirit, soul and body) to every*

*person who has used me as a victim. I ask you to remove all shock, fear, trauma and terror from my body, soul and spirit that came as a result of being victimized by anyone. I also ask you to cleanse all land and time defiled during the time I was being victimized. I break all ungodly bonding to the location where it happened. I declare that I am no longer a victim but I am an over-comer through The Name of The Lord Jesus Christ. Amen!*

Over the next few months Mary ministered to Sonja and helped her recognize the lies she had believed about herself and others, as well as the judgments and vows she had made as a result.

By the time the police released her to go home; she had found a greater measure of freedom than she had previously known. As a survivor of human trafficking; she knew and had determined in her heart that she would get the necessary training and education to help others who had, or would go through what she had suffered. She was no longer a victim, but an over-comer, and was committed to live as a victor.

## Chapter Ten

# My route to freedom

Patterns or cycles in your life often indicate that you may need healing in that particular area. When you continually have similar circumstances occurring in your life, it could be that you have some unhealed hurts and, unresolved issues needing attention.

When you are in the midst of a recurring pattern, you should pay attention to the emotions you are experiencing at that time. You must ask yourself some questions about what you believe about God, about others, and about yourself.

As you get in touch with the emotions you feel through the experience, Invite God into the midst of your emotions and ask Him the very first time in your life that you felt this way. Do not try to figure it out in your mind, but let it bubble up out of your heart. Next allow what you believed about yourself, others, and God, at that time to surface in your heart.

The beliefs of the initial incident are often similar to what is believed in the most current incident, but might also have a core belief about your character such as: I am unworthy, I am to blame, I am guilty, to name a few.

Often the feeling is that God was not there to protect you, or He was there, and chose to let it happen, He just stood by and watched. You judged God as untrustworthy and as a result, made a decision or vow to protect yourself or hide-away and shut down. When you self protect, you decide to take control and become the master of your own life and destiny. You kicked God off the throne of your heart.

When you discover "I am" statements inside your heart, it is usually a place where you have displaced God, The Great I Am, and made yourself a god in the situation. When you make a vow to self protect, you build a wall around your heart to keep yourself safe and prevent future hurt.

The problem is when you put up a wall, it also keeps God and others out, and you create a stronghold for the enemy. You have, though your own self-protection, and through your agreement with the father of lies, created a throne for him to sit on.

As long as you agree with the lies and false identities about yourself, as well as the judgments and vows made about others and God; the enemy has a legal right to occupy the throne in that hardened part of your heart.

In order to displace the enemy you have to break your agreement with him. Satan is the father of deception and hides behind the lies in your heart.

If you knew you were deceived, you no longer would be. Because you are deceived, you need some help to identify the lies hidden deep within you. Unfortunately you have a wall of self-protection which keeps the truth hidden even from yourself. The only way of escape is inviting God to come inside the wall of protection you have erected, to do the work in you and for you. God is faithful to come inside when you ask, and will dismantle the structure the enemy has been hiding inside of. He will also do it in a way and a timing that you can handle.

While reading through this book, you may have found that you had memories of your own that need healing. The Personal Workbook beginning on page 102 was designed to help you to reach deep into your heart for the memories that will bring your breakthrough. As you work your way through your memory, please be careful to take note of all your feelings, as they will lead you to the truth of what you really believe.

Once you have identified your own personal lies, judgments and vows, then you can follow the workbook outline to come to a place of knowing and confessing the truth as God sees it.

Maintaining your freedom will be a process of monitoring your feelings and thinking from that point on. The enemy of your soul will often attempt to get you to believe the same lies, make the same judgments as you had done previously. Therefore, you must be on guard for a period of time to watch what triggers you with the same emotions and thinking. I stress a period of time, as we do not want to be eternal naval gazers.

## Chapter Eleven

# PERSONAL WORKBOOK

Personal Workbook

# **Personal Worksheets for Self Discovery**

*A user friendly way to enable you to demolish the enemy's stronghold in your heart.*

Give a brief description of the patterns or cycles causing your **current problem**:

*abuse - not building walls, not loving myself. Repeated abuse -*

**Feeling statements:**

Feeling Statements are important in uncovering what you really believe in any situation. If you cannot immediately access what you **believe**, you can access how you **felt** in the situation. Looking at the issue you recorded above, write down the emotions you feel below: (*If you have a problem defining your emotions check the **Feeling Words list** at the end of the book*).

I feel _____ (e.g. angry, lonely, unworthy)
I am _____ (e.g. alone, misunderstood)
I can't _____ (e.g. move forward)

**OTHERS** are/will _hurt, betray, abuse_
(E.g. untrustworthy, abusive, or will hurt, betray, leave you)

**GOD** is/was _absent, let things happen_
(E.g. absent, there but not involved, untrustworthy)

**Therefore** I will/must _protect myself - shut down_
(E.g. hide, protect myself, shut down, disappear)

**From the above you can clearly define what lies you have believed. Fill them in below**

**Lies believed as a result of the current problem:**

About Self: My family doesn't love me. I am not of value in my family. I do not fit in my family.

About others: didn't love me just wanted me for sex

About God: God did not protect me from the sexual abuse or emotional abuse / anger does

# Personal Workbook

**Description of <u>earliest memory</u>** related to emotions connected to the above listed lies.

*(Question to ask God: When was the first time I believed these lies or felt these feelings?)*

Sexual abuse by Harry
I felt used, unworthy, unloved, low, dirty & disgusting

*(Complete the Feeling Statement exercise again for the earliest memory)*

## <u>Lies related to earliest memory:</u>

About Self: I must have deserved it. I wanted attention & got wrong attention as usual. I should never have been born.

About Others: They should have paid attention to me & would not have happened to me.

About God: If he loved me he would have protected me. God was not the God if he would let that happen

*When dealing with wounds to our souls, we need to look for certain issues that are present in most incidents:*

## UNFORGIVENESS

Forgiveness needs to be given and received towards God, towards others and towards ourselves. If you cannot think about the offence without pain or anger, there is most likely unforgiveness present.

**ACTION**: Ask God to show you who you need to forgive. We need to forgive the offender, but often there are others who could have prevented the incident and we need to forgive them also.

## JUDGEMENTS

First, there will be **judgments** made about ourselves, others and God; as well as subsequent **vows** made because of these judgments.

**ACTION:** The power of the judgments and vows need to be broken; then we must ask God to stop all sowing and reaping cycles in your life from these vows and judgments. Next, all the demonic power assigned to keep the judgments and vows in place need to be dismissed in The Name of Jesus Christ.

### SHOCK/FEAR/TRAUMA

There will be **physiological** affects to our body as well as **impact** on the heart, mind, and spirit.

Shock fear and trauma and sometimes even terror can be lodged in our body and nervous system. This needs to be removed. Only God can heal us in these areas.

**ACTION:** Take authority over the Shock/Fear/Trauma/Terror associated with the incident, and command it out of and off the body. Next ask God to heal every part of your being, and bring your spirit/soul/body into alignment in The Name of Jesus Christ. Ask God to turn off the hyper vigilance in your nervous system and adjust and balance all chemicals within your body.

### UNGODLY CONNECTIONS

**Ungodly connections** between the abused and abuser, as well as the location of the abuse need to be severed. Additionally all defilement needs to broken off the land and time where the incident occurred.

**ACTION**: Break every ungodly spirit/soul/body tie between yourself and the offender. You must also break every ungodly attachment to the location of the offence. Break defilement off of the land and time especially where there was blood loss or sexual sins or idolatry committed, as well as broken covenants.

Where the soul is held captive we must ask God to move us from the **Prison** – our *place of captivity*, to the **Palace** – our *position of authority* that we hold in Christ Jesus according to Ephesians 2:6. *"And raised us up together, and made us sit together in the heavenly places in Christ Jesus."*

## **ACTION TO TAKE:**

1. You must ask God to come into the **Prison** – the captive area of your heart - beyond your own self protective walls and hardened heart.

2. You must dethrone the enemy of your soul who you made covenant with through the lies you believed, and judgements and vows made as a result.

3. Ask Jesus to take up residence in the vacated area of your heart and fill you with His Holy Spirit.

4. Ask God to take the part of you held captive and place you in heavenly places in Christ Jesus, the **Palace** - your place of immunity and authority.

*Note*:  *A simple checklist is always handy to ensure that we cover all the areas necessary to bring a person into complete healing and recovery.*

### ✓ **Issue Covered**

- ☐ Forgiveness: God, Others, and Self
- ☐ Confess & Break Judgments of God
- ☐ Confess & Break Judgments of Others
- ☐ Confess & Break Judgments of Self
- ☐ Break all Vows & Covenants
- ☐ Remove Shock, Fear, Trauma, Terror
- ☐ Break all Ungodly ties and connections
- ☐ Invite Jesus into the Prison in your heart
- ☐ Dethrone the enemy from your heart
- ☐ Enthrone Jesus in your heart
- ☐ Ask to be Filled with The Holy Spirit
- ☐ Take the captive from the Prison to the Palace
- ☐ Dismiss all demonic trespassers

## **Prayer of Deliverance**

*Father, God of Abraham, I am unable in my own strength to pull down the protective walls that I have erected around my heart. I now invite You into my heart and behind this wall to enable me first to will, and then do, what is needed to break my agreement with the enemy.*

*I choose to forgive (name the offender(s)) _____ for their sin against me that caused me to believe these lies and make the judgments and vows I made as a result. I agree that by forgiving _____ it will no longer be charged to their account on Your great judgment day.*

*I break all the resulting ungodly connections to _____, as well as all ungodly attachments to the location of the offence(s). I ask you to break defilement off the land and time of the offense, as well as all shock, fear, trauma or terror binding me to it.*

*I break the power of all judgments I made of: _____ (Others you judged), that they were_____*

*I also break the power of all vows I made as a result of these judgments (state vows).*

*I ask You, Father God, to forgive me for believing these lies and for making the resulting judgments and vows. Please break all curses as well as reaping and sowing patterns and cycles that came into my life as a consequence. I pray this in the Name of Jesus Christ, my Lord.*

*Lord I ask you to evict the enemy from his hiding place and take the throne he has occupied. As King David cried in Psalm 142; I now cry: "Take my soul out of prison, that I might praise Your Name".*

*I now command the enemy along with all his power and evil forces to leave me. I cut myself free from all principalities, powers, titles dominions, and covenants that had a legal right over my life as a result.*

*Lord I ask you to cleanse that part of me that was held captive and now take it and seat it with You in heavenly places, that I might take* **my true position in Christ**. *Amen!*

### Ephesians 2:6-7 (AMP)

*"And He raised us up together with Him and made us sit down together (giving us "joint seating with Him) in the heavenly sphere (by virtue of our being) in Christ Jesus (the Messiah, the Anointed One) He did this that He might clearly demonstrate through the ages to come the immeasurable (limitless, surpassing) riches of His free grace (His unmerited favor) in (His) kindness and goodness towards us in Christ Jesus*

# FEELING WORDS

| | | |
|---|---|---|
| Abandoned | Inhibited | Put down |
| Abused | Insecure | Rejected |
| Accused | Insignificant | Resented |
| Afraid | Insulted | Restricted |
| Alone | Interrogated | Ridiculed |
| Ashamed | Intimidated | Robbed |
| Attacked | Invaded | Scared |
| Blamed | Invalidated | Shamed |
| Brushed off | Invisible | Shameful |
| Cheated | Judged | Skeptical |
| Confused | Labeled | Slandered |
| Controlled | Left out | Suffocated |
| Criticized | Lied about | Suspicious |
| Cut down | Lied to | Teased |
| Defensive | Lonely | Terrified |
| Dehumanized | Manipulated | Threatened |
| Disapproved of | Misjudged | Trapped |
| Disbelieved | Misled | Unappreciated |
| Discouraged | Mistrusted | Uncared for |
| Disrespected | Mistrusting | Unheard |
| Embarrassed | Misunderstood | Unimportant |
| Fearful | Mocked | Uninformed |
| Forced | Neglected | Uninvited |
| Frightened | Obligated | Unknown |
| Guarded | Offended | Unloved |
| Guilty | Offended | Unprotected |
| Humiliated | Over-protected | Unsafe |
| Inadequate | Over-ruled | Unsupported |
| Ignored | Powerless | Unwanted |
| Imposed upon | Pressured | Unworthy |
| Imprisoned | Punished | Violated |
| Inferior | Pushed down | Worthless |

*Juanita Lubin* has ministered both as a conference speaker and seminar and workshop leader in Canada and internationally. She speaks on various subjects including:

- ❖ Freedom from Freemasonry
- ❖ Prophetic Intercession
- ❖ The Feasts of Israel
- ❖ Spiritual Gifts

However, Juanita's heart message continues to be "setting the captive free from, the chains of the enemy".

For more information please contact:

jaellighthouse@gmail.com

905-673 1716

Made in the USA
Charleston, SC
21 February 2013